TOOLS FOR CAREGIVERS

- **F&P LEVEL:** B
- **WORD COUNT:** 23
- **CURRICULUM CONNECTIONS:** machines

Skills to Teach

- **HIGH-FREQUENCY WORDS:** a, an, big, has, is, it
- **CONTENT WORDS:** arm, backhoe, buckets, build, dig(s), drives, dumps, helps, lifts
- **PUNCTUATION:** exclamation point, periods
- **WORD STUDY:** /k/, spelled ck (backhoe, buckets); long /o/, spelled oe (backhoe); short /i/, spelled i (big, dig, is, it, lifts)
- **TEXT TYPE:** information report

Before Reading Activities

- Read the title and give a simple statement of the main idea.
- Have students "walk" through the book and talk about what they see in the pictures.
- Introduce new vocabulary by having students predict the first letter and locate the word in the text.
- Discuss any unfamiliar concepts that are in the text.

After Reading Activities

Flip back through the book with readers. Ask them to point out each word that has a short /i/ vowel sound. What other short vowel sounds do they read in the book?

Tadpole Books are published by Jump!, 5357 Penn Avenue South, Minneapolis, MN 55419, www.jumplibrary.com

Copyright ©2025 Jump. International copyright reserved in all countries. No part of this book may be reproduced in any form without written permission from the publisher.

Editor: Jenna Gleisner **Designer:** Emma Almgren-Bersie

Photo Credits: Alekcey/Shutterstock, cover; DarthArt/iStock, 1; Photobac/Dreamstime, 2tl, 2tr, 4–5; nazarovsergey/Shutterstock, 2ml, 14–15; Chet_W/iStock, 2mr, 6–7; Dmitry Kalinovsky/Shutterstock, 2bl, 2br, 8–9, 12–13; bogubogu/Shutterstock, 3; Another77/Shutterstock, 10–11; Dmitry Kalinovsky/Dreamstime, 16.

Library of Congress Cataloging-in-Publication Data
Names: Gleisner, Jenna Lee, author.
Title: Backhoes / by Jenna Lee Gleisner.
Description: Minneapolis, MN: Jump!, Inc., [2025]
Series: Machines on the move | Includes index.
Audience: Ages 3–6
Identifiers: LCCN 2024021020 (print)
LCCN 2024021021 (ebook)
ISBN 9798892135832 (hardcover)
ISBN 9798892135849 (paperback)
ISBN 9798892135856 (ebook)
Subjects: LCSH: Backhoes—Juvenile literature. | Excavating machinery—Juvenile literature.
Classification: LCC TA735 .G557 2025 (print)
LCC TA735 (ebook)
DDC 629.225—dc23/eng/20240513
LC record available at https://lccn.loc.gov/2024021020
LC ebook record available at https://lccn.loc.gov/2024021021

MACHINES ON THE MOVE

BACKHOES

by Jenna Lee Gleisner

TABLE OF CONTENTS

Words to Know 2

Dig 3

Let's Review! 16

Index 16

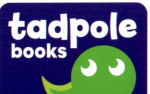

WORDS TO KNOW

arm

buckets

build

digs

dumps

lifts

DIG

A backhoe is big.

It has an arm.

bucket

It has buckets.

It digs!

It lifts.

It drives.

It dumps.

It helps build.

LET'S REVIEW!

Backhoes are big machines! They help us build. What is this backhoe doing?

INDEX

arm 4
big 3
buckets 5
build 15

digs 7
drives 11
dumps 13
lifts 9